THE DREAM UNFURLED

A Manifesto
for
Millennial
America

by

Cory D. Maley

The Dream Unfurled: A Manifesto for Millennial America

Photo of the author by Michele Giardina and Robert Cerrato.

Published by Hats Off Books®
610 East Delano Street, Suite 104
Tucson, Arizona 85705 U.S.A.
www.hatsoffbooks.com

Publisher's Cataloging-in-Publication
(Provided by Quality Books, Inc.)

Maley, Cory D.
  The dream unfurled : a manifesto for millennial America/ by Cory D. Maley.
  p. cm.
  ISBN 1587363755
  LCCN 2004110144

  1. United States--Politics and government.
2. Ideology--United States. 3. United States--Economic conditions. 4. United States--Social conditions.
5. Social values--United States. 6. Human rights--United States. I. Title.

JK31.M35 2004   320.973
                       QBI04-700335

For all the children of the Earth
who will inherit the legacy of Res Publica

Acknowledgments

"Silent gratitude isn't much use to anyone."

— G. B. Stern

I have daydreamed about how to improve our systems of governance for as long as I can remember knowing what the word meant. It is a strange thing for a teenager to have even considered in passing, much less to have spent much time contemplating; that preoccupation has not been lost in the many years that have passed since then. Yet, what has changed is the depth of my convictions—so much so that I feel I must speak out for the changes I have so long considered. While it is my name that dances across the cover, I could not have produced this work without the help and support of a great many people who have made indelible marks upon my life, mind, and numerous drafts of this manuscript.

First and foremost, let me thank my parents, from whom I benefited not simply a generous, safe, and loving childhood, but also their examples as human beings. From my dad I have learned so much about the power of building people up through fairness, strength, and dignity; he demonstrated time and again the importance of doing what is right, not what is easy, and to never turn a blind eye away from what is wrong if you have the power to make it right, even if it is unpopular. From my mom I have learned a great deal about the power of kindness and perception. She has an uncanny ability to find what is good in people and to make that her prime connection with them. I can only imagine the goodwill a world full of people with her keen eye and strong heart could produce. To be sure, this is the prime attribute of a uniter that I strive to emulate.

Second, I owe a debt of gratitude to the University of Calgary and Stanford University for the impeccable educational opportunities they afforded me. I am especially indebted to Holger Herwig, Shadia Drury, and Barry Cooper. While I'm not sure the latter person will appreciate the content of this book, I must nonetheless extend my gratitude to these three professors, under whose tutelage I learned to think, argue, question, and above all maintain a coherent vision. Moreover, they drove me to succeed by fostering my skills and refusing to accept mediocre writing from me when they knew I was capable of more sophisticated work. Without them I could not have hoped to achieve in my life what I have so far succeeded in accomplishing.

Without the numerous contributions of my friends and family members who slogged through endless copies of this work as it evolved, it would have been a far inferior work. The world does not have thanks enough to express my gratitude. Their ideas, contribution, criticisms, suggestions, and editing prowess have so altered my original draft that it cannot be said to be at all the same except in spirit. As you read, I ask you to recognize that this is not solely my creation, but the inner workings of many who have found the time and energy to contribute, each in their own way. Thank-you to my girlfriend Helen, brother Darren, sister Connie, my auntie Colleen, and friends and coworkers Zorina, Wendy, Shelly, Derek, Dave, Derry, and Grant, whose help and variety of contributions I could not have done without. I owe a special debt of gratitude to my friends Dan and Alan, who read, reread, critiqued, and helped me to formulate my ideas in a coherent fashion; without their support and wisdom you would not now be reading this book.

Finally, I must thank my students, who have touched my life in ways they will likely never realize. I have such trepidation, and yet still greater hope for their futures and those of their families to come, that I cannot not turn a blind eye to what is possible.

They have such concern that the world does not represent them, and yet are so often resigned to swallow it whole anyway. It is because of them that I feel I must say with total seriousness: a new world is possible, we just have to make it work.

Preface

"We cannot become what we need to be
by remaining what we are."

— Max DePree

As the oldest constitutional republic in the world, America has been, and in many ways still is, a beacon of hope. I believe it is essential that we take it upon ourselves to ensure that it continues to be so. America, as an ideal, represents the world as it could be, so it is little wonder that so many around the world choose to immigrate here from countries around the globe as I have done; to the industrialized and underdeveloped, the rich and poor, the young and old alike, the American dream, the desire for a better tomorrow, is a powerful lure. To a great extent, America has not failed to deliver the goods, so to speak. This nation's progress has contributed to increased political and social freedom, peace, and prosperity for its inhabitants. Yet, if we allow ourselves and our country to indulge in a self-congratulatory and complacent stupor, then we shall have much to lose. If the world ceases to look up to us, then it will not be long before they look down upon us.

It is ignorant, and, indeed, arrogant to believe that we have reached the final stages of our development. We mustn't presume that today's social, political, and economic systems represent the pinnacle of social evolution. Where we stand today is but a rung on the ladder of human development, albeit the one we are currently holding onto. The assurance that we have so nearly reached the top that very little effort needs to be expended to reach it is a false one. Indeed, we have so much yet to do that I hardly think we can even see the rung for which we are striving except perhaps in our imagination.

We all have an image in our minds about what America is meant to be, what it is supposed to represent; there are as many differing viewpoints about this as there are people. Yet one thing that most Americans can agree upon is that the government is meant to be made up of the people, be selected by the people, and act in accordance with the best interests of the people. It is a fundamental tenet of the United States we have come to know and love. But no matter how much we believe in this notion of governance of, by, and for the people, it is not, and cannot be, a reality unless we, the people, work to ensure that American governance and democracy do indeed function this way.

While I believe that there is truth in the old adage that change starts at home, I must respectfully disagree that this is what will solve the problems facing this country. Change at home will not resolve the systematic weaknesses this nation faces today. The paradigm shift that so many Americans desire toward a more equitable, more peaceful, more democratic country must begin with a fundamental revision in the way that the institutions of our country administer its development; the change must begin with the alteration of American governance. In propelling this shift in consciousness it is the people, and only the people, who have the power to rise up and demand such change.

It is my sincere hope that this treatise will prompt you to action in the remaking of this country and the world in which we find ourselves, and not, as so often is the case, prove so daunting a undertaking that you do nothing. The greatness of the United States is found not in the fact that it is the richest country in the world, nor that it has unparalleled military might. On the contrary, what makes this country great is that we have every right to demand that the government act in accordance with our principled desires rather than have the government's agenda shoved down our throats. We have, quite simply, allowed this to occur for far too long and it is high time that we do something about it.

I feel altogether blessed to live in the United States because it is a country with great promise. But I do not let my pride blind me to what it has become. When I look at this country, I see so much potential and yet so much that is left wanting. It is at once the richest, most powerful nation on the planet, and yet it has the highest percentages of imprisoned, medically uninsured or underinsured, and impoverished citizens in the industrialized world. Clearly this has not been the result of our inabilities to fix these problems; we are a creative people and have no shortage of resources with which to solve our problems. Rather, it is indicative of the misguided priorities of our leaders and our unwillingness to do anything about it.

Thus, it is in no way my intent to slander America, for it is indeed a great nation, one deserving of admiration and respect. Yet, if it is to remain a venerable body in the eyes of humankind, I believe it is of the utmost urgency that we reconcile ourselves to the fact that there are important undertakings we must attend to in order to bring about the changes necessary to rectify those problematic areas of our economy, society, and government. Only when we embark upon this endeavor honestly and earnestly can we begin to remake our country anew. Together we can, and will, reclaim American democracy and governance for the people, to whom it rightfully belongs.

A Promise Still Unfulfilled

"Undertake not what you cannot perform,
but be careful to keep your promise."

— George Washington

There is a growing concern in this country that the government, institutions, and even the law are no longer serving the country as they should; they do not represent the greater interests of society or the common weal of the people. There is a sliding decline in political involvement, coupled with an ever-increasing political disaffection, grounded in the belief that the system serves only a privileged few while it ignores the vast majority of people in this country. Interestingly, this sentiment rings true of people whose interests span the entire political spectrum. Be they conservative or liberal, there is a growing body of people who, despite their complacency, desire change. That desire is beginning to percolate into action in America. The time, it seems, has come for a new progressive age—a peaceful revolution of millennial proportions toward becoming a society in which every member has the resources, support, and opportunities with which to realize their highest potential.

Our current paradigm is dying, albeit slowly, as a result of its own momentum. Up until now we have been pillaging the planet and its people in the name of production, advancement, progress, civilization, and industry. The dominant mode of thought of the all-too-recent past has been to take solace in the notion that the consumption of the present will be replaced by the bounty of our future. We have hedged our bets upon the generations of our unknown descendants with ample confidence that they will succeed where we have failed: they will repair the world from the afflictions of generations past. But the recent fomentation of ideas in our country has called this conventional wisdom, if it can be called such, into question. Will we have the time and compunction to deliver ourselves from this peril, or will the momentum we have gained make it impossible for us to accept anything but our collective annihilation?

The answer, simply, is that we cannot know. Will our children have the willpower to overcome the vices that we have been unwilling—and as a result unable—to purge from our worldview? Again, we cannot know until, ultimately, it is too late. And while we have for centuries recognized that living our individual lives so as to avoid planning for our future survival is both foolish and beyond contempt, we permit our societies to develop and act in just such a manner. Niccolo Machiavelli cautioned his readers in *The Prince* not to test their luck with fortune, for those who do are always, in time, the loser in the end. To paraphrase his warning: fate's a bitch; and I, for one, am unwilling to place the development and future of our people in the hands of gamblers, fools, and blind men, nor am I willing to pawn off our responsibility to generations yet to be conceived.

What I desire most is to live a happy, fulfilling, healthy, and prosperous life, one through which I can realize my highest potential free of oppression, violence, and hatred. I am not alone in my wont. We have been told for a great many years that these conditions are already available to us, that our system is providing us with the tools to achieve this aim. People are rapidly realizing that instead, our system has merely furnished our lives with a false sense that the good life is on the horizon. Far from approaching the horizon, however, many Americans find that they are rapidly losing sight of it as it pulls further and further away from their purview. Furthermore, there are those in society with vested interests in the present state of affairs who will resist relinquishing their power and control over the future of the system; indeed, they resist the future as a whole, for it is in their interest to maintain the present in perpetuity. In any society, the established structures that are produced by certain groups also serve to benefit these groups, even if they represent a relatively minor proportion of the general population.

As a result of these structures, these groups frequently become disproportionately rich and powerful in relation to others in that society. Thus, it is not without difficulty that the radical alteration of our path will be undertaken; great deeds, though they be full of rewards, are never without sacrifice nor faced without trepidation. Our system has been molded in such a way that it serves to repel progressive change and to roll back previous developments. Failing this, it aims to maintain the status quo. Upon the political spectrum, this characteristic nature would place our system right of center. That is not to say that it is Republican in nature. I do not believe that the Democrats and Republicans can so readily be divided along such lines. On the contrary, the distinction between Right and Left has less to do with political parties than it does with the direction we desire to take the country, that is, if we are going to move it at all. Richard Rorty points out that the Left sees the country's development as "still to be achieved," whereas the Right holds that this process is already complete and should be preserved, or should recede into the past.

Let me provide an example that I hope will serve to clarify this point. Liberals and conservatives are quick to identify each other as leftist or rightist, respectively; and while there is a rough correlation between liberalism and the Left, and conservatism and the Right, this identification is not altogether accurate, given that what it means to be a member of the political Right or Left has to do with how one views progress with relation to the past and future. The "center" on the Left-Right spectrum is considerably right of center in relation to the liberal-conservative spectrum. Thus, many people who can be clearly identified as conservative cannot necessarily be considered rightist. Take the popular Bill O'Reilly of *The O'Reilly Factor* fame: Liberals decry O'Reilly as a Right-wing conservative, and O'Reilly may even feel that way himself, but this is a misconception and misuse of the terminology. While it is true that O'Reilly is a conservative—of that their can be no contention—his beliefs fall left of center on the Left-Right continuum. He writes in his book *The No-Spin Zone* that liberals consider him Lucifer "because I don't feel guilty about societal ills. Hell, I'm *trying* to improve things." In this he is most correct.

Do not feel guilty about what others before us have done; there is no benefit or practicality in this. Guilt paralyzes; we need action. We are not guilty; we are responsible—responsible for righting past mistakes, responsible for the present, and responsible to the generations that will carry on or suffer because of our legacy. After reading his books, it is clear to me that Bill O'Reilly sees that America's development has yet to be realized, and is thus a part of the political Left, conservative though he may be. This is not to say that the many Right-wingers are not also trying to change something, but to the "Right" this change is in regard to an ideal in the past, be it real or imagined; "the good ol' days," as it were. Conservatives merely take a different tack on how we will achieve future than do liberals.

This is why I rail against the conservative-as-rightist versus the liberal-as-leftist duality; it is misleading and serves little more than to divide us into factions that are not altogether that different from each other, at least not irreconcilably so. This division leverages the power away from the American people and into the hands of the power elite. More than 2,500 years ago, Sun Tzu wrote in *The Art of War* that the best way to persevere in battle is to divide your opponent's forces.

In the battle for supremacy over the American ideal, when the whole is divided against itself it may indeed continue to stand but it certainly cannot walk. If one wished to maintain control of the power structure of this country, it would be crucially important that the people of this country remained divided so that the powers-that-be could not be challenged. This is so even if, and perhaps especially if, it occurs through the erroneous division of liberals and conservatives. For when we mistakenly believe that we are not on the same side, we will always have the other as an antagonist and scapegoat for which to blame our problems on, rather than a partner with which to solve them.

The polarization of the Left and Right is therefore unproductive at best, and at its worst it is factious and counterproductive. Yet while many of us may in fact have more in common than we thought we did, I do see that the current positioning of American politics is to the right of center, and this I see as problematical. What is problematic in this predisposition is that such a political climate not only hinders progressive change, but also fosters the propensity toward rescinding the progress we have made up to now. The environment, civil rights, corporate conduct, labor, family values, economic prudence, and financial independence are all being eroded by the current climate of American governance.

Conservatives and liberals alike are dissatisfied, if you will excuse the understatement, with the nation's present state of affairs. And if you will notice, the issues Americans often hold in opposition to one another are inherently tied together. When labor is devalued and corporations are allowed to misuse and abuse workers, traditional family values fall apart; both parents feel they need to work in order to make ends meet, and because of this stress many families fall into debt. What is more, the number one cause of marital stress is family finance. Conservative and liberal interests are not inherently opposed, they are inextricably linked.

So who is benefiting from this factious environment; who is the American Right if not the conservative faction? It is the American power class—most notably corporate America—that is reaping the benefits of the status quo. More than anyone else that covets this ideological bent, the power elite threatens to dam off the regular progression of ideological currents in order to maintain its station in the relative calm of a system that serves to benefit them disproportionately. Furthermore, because the system benefits the power elite, who make up the vanguard of the political Right, they fear, as Rorty points out, economic and political change. As such, when the politics of the nation finds itself in the current alignment, the nation's policies and indeed our future are in danger of being hijacked. Progressive developments that protect people from the power elite are held in place by only the most gossamer of anchors. As Rorty suggests, when this ideological paradigm is pervasive the government is highly susceptible to being subordinated to the role of "pawn of the rich and powerful," whose self-interest is "served by forestalling such change." With the two most powerfully *active* forces in the political machinery, namely the government and the power elite, devoted to preserving the country's current mode of being, the great vehicle of change in our society stalls in the driveway of progress, leaving us stranded and seemingly abandoned in the process before it has even begun.

Still, it is not so simple as to say the rich and powerful are oppressing everyone else. There is no roomful of CEOs plotting the demise of the middle and working classes, and I have an extraordinarily difficult time with any notion that the upper echelons of society have, on the whole, any more malevolence about them in how they look upon the rest of the country than any other grouping of Americans. I cannot help but think that such claims are hysterical in nature. On the contrary, for those in control of the system of power, their tendencies do not lie in any active malevolence; rather, the affluent classes' resistance to change resides in their desire to maintain the privileges they enjoy. For this I cannot blame them, for it seems only natural that people would desire, if not to improve their station in society, at least to maintain it.

This may seem like a minor distinction, but it is an important one. In our current situation, the rich and powerful who benefit most from the system desire the status quo to remain the prevailing paradigm precisely because it is beneficial for them. In all honesty, who can doubt the rationality of this disposition; when you are at the top of the socioeconomic pyramid, the only likely change that can come to fruition through a transformation of the power structure is the diminution of that station. At least this is how it must appear from that vantage point. However, the situation is not exactly a zero-sum gain whereby when the rich lose the poor gain, or when the poor gain the rich lose. There is a very real extent to which the rising tide raises all ships. Still, there is a very important caveat here; when the tide rises in such a way that some waves ascend enormously, while others dip to an extreme nadir, the result is a perilous storm whereby only the largest of ocean liners may traverse it with ease while the junks and sailboats are tossed and crushed by the squalls.

Regardless of how much the upper echelons of society may have paralyzed social, political, and economic change in our country in one sense, they have mobilized it in another; the great many philanthropical endeavors of the wealthy that are predicated upon the betterment of society have provided the undergirding for the new American renaissance. Far from being the enemy, America's affluent and the powers that represent American enterprise have the potential to be our nation's greatest benefactors. It is, furthermore, a fundamental detriment to any cause or movement to create a dichotomy in which the rich are viewed as the oppressors, and everyone else the victims of their oppression. There is little purpose that can be served by alienating this sector of society.

When we partake in class-oriented estrangement we create a paradigm that precludes any form of change that espouses the cooperation of the rich and powerful—that is unless one wishes to embrace the violent overthrow of the system that Karl Marx propounded in his *Communist Manifesto*. I have grave doubts that such a course of action would result in anything but another form of systematic oppression. After all, communism as we have experienced it in the twentieth century has shown itself to be altogether oppressive in its own right. And while I concede that Marx would regard communism as it has been manifested as a gross aberration of his ideal, his own ideology was not free from violence and oppression. In the inevitable overthrow of the bourgeoisie by the proletariat, he concluded that the bourgeoisie would have to be destroyed if they could not agree to the formation of a communist society, whereby they, too, would become part of the proletariat. I can no more accept the destructive tyranny of the multitudes over the oligarchs than I can the stifling tyranny of oligarchs over the multitudes.

We must, therefore, be careful to avoid such a dangerous dichotomization of our people. Indeed, for the promise of a better tomorrow, we must be willing to relinquish our previously held notions that rely upon simplistic dualities. In the same breath, I also understand their powerful allure; they are attractive in their simplicity. For, if we live in a black-and-white world then there is very little to think about: If I am right, and I am assured that this is so, then the person who disagrees with me must by extension be wrong. It is easier to grapple with than the possibility that we might both be either right or wrong, or that we might have to reconcile ourselves with the notion that what is truly correct might be some combination of both, or a multitude of, ideas. Political philosopher Carl Schmitt argues in his *Political Romanticism* that every "clear antithesis exercises a dangerous power of attraction over other distinctions that are not as clear." Most prevalent among these antitheses is that of good and evil.

Notions of good and evil are frequently employed in times of crisis; it stifles debate and doubt when a nation wants nothing more than action and clarity. America is no stranger to the deployment of such tactics. Take, for instance, the rhetoric of President George W. Bush vis-à-vis the rest of the world regarding the war in Iraq. While Bush's *you're either with us or against us* duality certainly produces a clear delineation between antipodean choices and eliminates any ambiguities, it functions as a threat and evasion of diplomacy, and it also serves to stifle the elements of an open society that lead us closer to the truth, not away from it. Truth will always be the first victim to black-and-white constructions.

Good and evil are perhaps our most fundamental dichotomy, but it is not especially useful to us; our view of what is good and what is evil is for all intents and purposes rather arbitrary. In his *Foundations of a Moral Life*, Baruch Spinoza warned that our notions of good and evil are really dependent upon factors outside of the moral judgment, namely good or evil itself. Furthermore, the only way that he could conceive that this moral judgment could be of positive use was to connect it to understanding. "We do not know," he wrote, "that anything is certainly good excepting that which actually conduces to understanding, and on the other hand, we do not know that anything is evil excepting that which can hinder us from understanding."

Although the simplicity of clear antitheses can be inviting, it will be our undoing if we allow it to persist as the dominant paradigm. Such dualities divert far too much energy away from more purposeful understandings because they are utterly superficial and thus they fall apart when they are considered in relation to reality without reinforcing them through artificial means; their construction simply does not allow, nor account, for the introduction of the ubiquitous varieties of our experience.

History has evinced time and again that ersatz constructions of understanding can only with great effort hold the profound power of revelatory experience at bay, and even then only for a time. It takes common vision and an honest search for understanding for us to even pose the questions that we need to ask, much less answer them. We cannot do this if we are intent upon making enemies of those with whom we do not agree. Our energies would be much better spent if we chose to devote them to the progression of ideals rather than the maintenance of a creature that lacks the legitimacy to survive in its own right.

Thus, it is my aim to produce an outcome that is consistent with the goal of becoming an understanding society, one which all of our people have the resources, support, and opportunities with which to realize their highest potential in this generation and those that will follow. The only "good" is that our decision promotes such a goal wholly, and the only "evil" is that it does not absolutely, and all that is in between these two poles must be weighed to determine to what extent decisions help or hinder the achievement of this goal. The answer, alone, is the only determinate of whether this policy is a good one or a bad one.

While at times it seems like a lot to ask that the promise of a better tomorrow be fulfilled, it surely is not impossible to achieve. In many ways we are incredibly intelligent, compassionate, creative beings and should we choose to actively pursue and develop our society in such a way that every individual has all the resources, support, and opportunities they need to achieve their highest potential, then surely we can do so. It is just that we must now take it upon ourselves to ensure that the broken promises of our generation shall not continue to fleece the children of future generations. We are but a small shift in consciousness away from radically altering the course we are plodding along into the future. Nietzsche declares in *Thus Spake Zarathushtra* that "Man is a rope stretched between the animal and the Superman—a rope over an abyss." It is a treacherous journey between our basest and highest selves, and today we struggle with "over-going[s]" and the "under-going[s]," taking the high road and the low road, in every step of our development.

The metaphor of the crossing is a powerful one, one with great relevance to us today. Imagine that our crossing is not an abyss, but a river. With each step along the rocks that dot the path from our animal selves to our sublime selves the water rises to wash over the rocks we have only just passed over, leaving in front of us ones that are soon to disappear themselves. Once we have moved beyond each step we may never turn back on the path from which we came. Each fateful step precludes undoing what we have done, and each step limits the future steps from which we may choose our path. We have little choice, but we still must choose from the myriad paths ahead how we ought to continue.

Yet today it is as if we are stepping upon our stones, looking only at our feet as we do so. We look only far enough ahead to see the stones upon which our feet are about to tread. It is a dreadful conclusion, I feel, that we may find ourselves at the end of our path, having only completed a part of our crossing. Such is the peril that we find ourselves in if we continue to grab forth at what is best in the short-term, be they profits, wars—what we gain from or destroy in them—exploitation, or otherwise, if we are careless about where we will be left in the long-term. It is only by raising up our eyes to behold the future steps, those of the many generations to follow us, that we may plan ahead to ensure that they may continue our crossing.

We have much to do to uplift our gaze, which has for so long transfixed itself only upon the outcomes of the immediate future. And though this will not be easy, we must do it for the good of the children who will inherit our Earth. Such an enormous undertaking simply cannot be accomplished without a shift in consciousness that transcends our desire for immediate gratification, be it as individuals or as a nation, in favor of a great and integrative set of interests that benefits the country, the world, and each individual within it for generations to come. And so it is with this charge that I am undertaking the writing of this treatise; it is my great hope that it will help to provide impetus for change, and that through it we may begin the journey of exploration that will remove the impediments to, and generate paths toward, the change that is necessary in order to realize the highest manifestation of this undertaking.

A Foundation for the Future

"The good of the people is the highest law."

— Cicero

"Justice is the end of government. It is the end of civil society. It ever has been and ever will be pursued until it be obtained, or until liberty be lost in the pursuit."

— James Madison

In order to properly address the issue of good governance we really must move beyond the simple, and often empty, calls for "less government" or "more democracy" in our country. In many ways, less government is as abhorrent as too much government. Thus changing the structure without changing the foundation or the materials from which it is built is really not a useful endeavor. A more meaningful query focuses on what the government is or does rather than how big it is or what it looks like. Because ultimately we cannot even begin to address these issues when we have not even established the basis for such an inquiry: what is the purpose of Government? It is a longstanding question in political philosophy and history alike, but that does not mean the question has been answered adequately.

Some philosophers claim the government is meant solely for upholding private contracts, while others assure us that it is set up to protect us from physical harm. Still others believe the government is meant to create a stable and prosperous environment for business development. Other visions of government project it as the harbinger of ideology to the world at large, be it globalization, Nazism, democracy, communism, religion, or what have you. There are even those who would deign to say that there should not be governments at all, and thus they should have no purpose whatsoever. But I feel that each of these are inadequate conceptions of what government ought to be and do. Not that they are necessarily wrong, but they do not adequately address what I see as being an issue of fundamental importance in determining the role of government: our individual and collective priorities. It is, most simply, a structure to produce that which is commonly agreed upon.

In order for us to determine what it is that we want the government to be or do, it is important for us to ask ourselves about our priorities. What do we want to accomplish and why is it important to us? The next question, then, is how can the government that we create help to facilitate the priorities we have decided upon? If we do not ask such questions, then it is as if we give the government a mandate of mayhem; in a system where there are no goals or prioritized parameters it is unlikely that the government will act in accordance with a set of unstated public goals. I would describe such a system of governance as the Calvinball theory of government.

In Bill Watterson's comic strip, *Calvin and Hobbes*, the two title characters play a game known as Calvinball. The game is characterized by the completely arbitrary and ephemeral nature of its goals and objectives. It is interesting to note that Calvin is always depicted as the weaker of the two, and is thus the least likely to succeed at Calvinball despite of, and perhaps even because of, the haphazard nature of the game. It is this disadvantage that eventually determines the completion of the game. It is not because Hobbes somehow manages to win, as there is no clear conclusion. Rather, it is simply that Calvin, who grows frustrated at his inability to overcome the systematic disadvantages he faces in the game, eventually becomes excessively upset, declares the whole game a farce, and quits. In this way nothing has been accomplished but that they have played the game for a number of hours.

In childhood this may in fact be the whole purpose of the game, namely to kill time on a sunny afternoon. But when considering governance structures, we would be remiss to say that the purpose of government is to simply "be the government" until some disadvantaged or disaffected group gets fed up with the system and overthrows it. To continue this line of comparison, such a situation leads only to a very slowly paced game of keep-away. One power governs for an unknown period of time until their possession of the governance system is wrested from them and guarded by another power. In this competition for political dominance over any given system, the public good is almost invariably sidelined.

Governments cannot afford to be so brash in marginalizing the public good, because in doing so it is impossible to avoid also marginalizing the governed public. Ultimately, if the government does not embrace and advocate for the governed, the governed will turn against it. In the game of keep-away described above, the governed are the wild card, so to speak, the fluid factor that can determine the outcome of the endeavor. If those in power ignore this factor, it can well be tapped by another force that would use it to its own advantage at the expense of the current authority.

An awful lot of energy must be expended under such a model to ensure that the fluid factor is contained because it is necessary to both mollify the people and prevent them from interfering in that structure. This impulse serves not only to constrain the governed vis-à-vis the government, but it also inhibits a society's ability to realize its full operational potential. So long as the system is such that those in charge of it must focus their energies upon shaping the public's perception so that the system may continue unmolested, there can be no effectual change.

In other words, when the system's dynamic is set up in such a way that the minds of the people have to be molded by the government in order for them to accept the principles of the system rather than allowing the system to be molded in accordance with the priorities that society sets for itself, the government ceases to be one of, by, and for the people. People become secondary to the state—a demand on the individual that is eerily reminiscent of the twentieth century's totalitarian regimes. On the other hand, in a system where the government is created to facilitate and support the attainment of goals that its society has prioritized, the society as a whole will experience greater actualization of that potential; there will be an increase in participation, productivity, creativity, and prosperity, among other benefits.

The foundation of democratic governance in the United States spoke to the ideal that the government may govern only at the behest of the people, that it is the people who should determine the policy and direction of the government by electing those who best reflect their priorities. I fear that the founding fathers would be aghast at the corporate hydra our government has become. Indeed, one of the reasons that the number of Americans who vote is on the decline is that they do not feel that the governing body addresses them or their priorities. On the contrary, they believe their voices have been hijacked, or at the very least drowned out, by corporate interests. While this situation is good for political parties, it is a serious problem if we are to maintain a robust democracy, and if we are to resolve it we need to address the issues that plague our system in an earnest and open manner. It is time that democracy be returned to its rightful guardians.

Shortly after the United States declared itself an independent republic, Thomas Paine wrote *Rights of Man*, arguing for the republican form of government. In it he explained that the word "republic" comes from the Latin phrase *res publica*, the public good, or "literally translated," he says, "the *public thing.*" According to Paine, the public good was to be the republican government's modus operandi, their whole purpose—to act on the behalf of the public good at the behest of the public. It was the people who would determine who was to govern and how they were to govern, and to set the agenda of those who performed the governing. The single most important determinant of a good government, he argued, was the degree to which the public good was held in high esteem.

To Paine, differentiating between a good government and a bad one was a distinction that was easily determined:

> Every Government that does not act on the principle of a Republic, or, in other words, that does not make the *res publica* its whole and sole object, is not a good Government. Republican Government is no other than Government established and conducted for the interest of the public, as well individually as collectively.

The problem with this model, however, is that it is often difficult for the government to see that it is not acting in accordance with the public good. The very idea that the government's purpose is to serve the public good is so ubiquitous and pervasive as an American ideal that the system does not permit those who guide it to acknowledge any other possibility.

It is my presumption that if I asked every politician on Capital Hill whether they were serving the public good or the good of a few private citizens, I am sure the response would be a resounding, if not unanimous, "I serve the public good." Furthermore, I would venture to say that those same politicians truly believe this to be the case. And yet, an overwhelming percentage of the adult population in the United States believes the exact opposite about whom the government serves. Clearly there is a disconnect in these disparate perceptions of the government.

Perhaps it is simply that the people of this country do not know what is good for them. I suppose the argument would come down in a Rousseauian fashion, namely that the public will can be mistaken. But I must admit, I am pretty suspicious of anyone who tells me that what I think is good for me really is not, and then attempts to convince me that what I really want is something that is actually far less good for me. Yet, the government, political parties, corporations, and individual politicians attempt to do this with relative consistency, and often they do so with great success. People consistently vote against their own interests owing to the clever sophistry of those who wish to solicit their support.

Imagine for a moment that I am a young adult who grew up in the projects, barrios, or a trailer park, suffering from the omnipresent concerns of drugs, violence, hunger, and discrimination that often penetrate such impoverished places. I have dropped out of school because I have had to work to help support my impoverished family. But because of my qualifications, or rather lack of them, I only make enough to subsist, so I do not make enough to go back to school to upgrade. Because of this I will not be able to qualify to go to a university to build the skills I need to improve my station. While there are indeed exceptions, and hard work and ingenuity can overcome great adversity, the exception does not detract from the harsh realities of the rule. And as such it is altogether probable that I will be caught in a cycle of poverty that is likely to play out with my children, just as it has for me.

Now, if I were asked what I thought the government's priorities should be I would be likely to tell them that I wanted financial help to support my family and to build the qualifications I needed to be successful in the future. Now envision a representative of the government coming to talk to me about my "mistaken understanding of the public good." They would like to convince me that the nation's security is a higher priority. With that said, they would tell me that there are no funds available for my conception of the good, because it would be allocated to the higher public good, namely, security projects such as the building of B-2 bombers, each costing taxpayers approximately $2.2 billion. Although my math skills may be a little weak, given the limited education I have had, I know that this is a lot of money, a lot more than would be required to lift my family and me out of poverty.

As a fifteen-year-old, I could work in a government-sponsored work program that provided education (high school and post-secondary) along the way, perhaps planting trees, painting, and maintaining dilapidated homes, or whatever the project may be, for the next ten years of my life. While I am doing this, they pay me $20,000 a year to help support my family, and let me assume that my educational and living expenses would cost an additional $40,000 annually. That total works out to be $60,000 annually. Let us even round it up to a $70,000 so that we can amply cover the cost of materials like saplings and paint. At the end of this program, the result is that my family's poverty has been alleviated, it has educated an individual to a great degree—which presumably will break the cycle of poverty—and the public has received ten years of public service in return. It is also likely that urban crime rates, drug abuse, poor health, and other poverty-induced conditions will have dropped for this family as a result of such a program. Further still, it is likely that this would have a rippling effect that would alleviate funding pressures in education, health, and crime prevention. But it has been costly; $70,000 annually. When one considers, however, that this program could be implemented for 31,428 individuals every year for the cost of a single B-2 bomber, one could conclude that the bomber is probably an inferior public good.

An argument can be made, however, that the bomber costing only $2.2 billion is most certainly a public good because its commissioning serves to protect the U.S. population of just over 290 million people for the low, low price of only $7.50 per capita. Furthermore, there are a great many jobs that are furnished by the defense sector. The development, production, and deployment of these bombers provides hundreds, if not thousands, of families with incomes that allow them to live comfortably. Given the choice between having no job and no income with which to support my family or to build bombers, the choice is obvious to me. It is a choice that has come to be known as a Hobbesian choice (named after the philosopher Thomas Hobbes, who discusses such choices at length in *Leviathan*), one between two alternatives where one of those alternatives is so unappealing (unemployment and poverty) that there is only one clear choice, even if it is also unappealing. Thus, there is a public good that is served by the B-2 bombers and the defense industry that makes its construction possible.

So the question becomes not about whether our choice serves a public good, per se, but rather, about what kind of public good we choose to pursue. What are the priorities that will determine the course we embark upon? Because, with every choice we make there are alternatives that we must forego. Such decisions will guide future choices about the nation we become, and its role in the future of our world. Certainly the decision-making process is infinitely more complex than a simple trade-off between two alternatives, as I have depicted above. Yet, it does serve to highlight the obvious range of possibilities that must lie between these two competing visions.

If on the one hand we choose to continue to spend the funds on military hardware, there are costs attached to it, just as there are costs attached to the choice to spend it on make-work projects. So what are we to do? What mitigating factors must we consider? The answer lies in our priorities, our vision. If we wish to create a more peaceful and prosperous society we must ask ourselves in an honest way, is the production of B-2 bombers the best way to promote peace and prosperity? It most certainly promotes prosperity, but the B-2 is not by any stretch of the imagination a "defensive" weapon, except perhaps in the doublespeak world of preemptive attacks. On the contrary, it is a weapon for purely offensive operations. With the alternative, there is a cost to the make-work projects insofar as the funds that were being used in making jobs for those who produce the B-2s will no longer be supporting them, and instead will be diverted to another priority, leaving them in the lurch (assuming these people would not be employed otherwise).

To look at the U.S. military budget, we see an allocation of $399.1 billion in 2002, which has since increased. If, as a nation, we decided that we would cut the military budget in half, it would stand at approximately $200 billion annually. It is interesting to note that such a budget would still be more extensive than Russia's, China's, Japan's, and Great Britain's (the next four big spenders) military budgets combined. That being said, this would provide approximately $200 billion annually to be spent elsewhere. If I, given my position as a young adult who grew up in a project, barrio, or trailer park decided that it would be best used if allocated to the program described above, I would be able to lift nearly three million young adults and their families out of poverty every year, and ultimately, it is possible that their condition would be alleviated permanently, given that those individuals would be provided with the irrevocable acquisition of an education. Now if I were given accurate information about the nature of government spending, and I looked around and all I ever saw was abject poverty, I would conclude that the government was mistaken about the public good, and not myself. For over thirty million Americans this understanding is not an abstract philosophical discourse, but a hard-to-swallow reality that they must face each day, without choice.

Of course, this is but one example. One could argue, moreover, that this is an extreme one that does not represent the public will any more than does the development of military hardware. There is a sense in this example that if the government spends its money there should be some productive gain for society. That is not to say that such a make-work program would not be productive; indeed, there is much to be gained from such endeavors, but there is not necessarily anything physically produced. If this is a concern, and it is debatable whether it ought to be, who is to say that we must produce military goods? After all, in order for the military manufacturing sector to remain productive the government must dispose of the weaponry it is producing so a new generation of weaponry may be produced. This, clearly, is an inherently destabilizing political force, not just for our country, but for the world at large.

There are innumerable other production-based endeavors that would better exemplify *res publica*, such as environmental technologies ranging from textiles to scrubbers, agriculture to fuels, and communications to space travel. The possibilities that better serve our people truly are endless. The greatest constraint is not a system of industrial production; the military-industrial complex would shift and adjust, as have the economies of the past. The change would not come without disruption, but that disruption will come whether we choose its arrival or not. I, for one, would much rather plan for this transition than to be run over by it. The primary obstacle to change is not economic in nature; rather, it is the political will to undertake this great shift in the American way of life.

Yet today the government spends and provides loopholes and pork that amounts to billions of dollars and by some estimates even trillions of dollars, on what is commonly described as corporate welfare, while many millions of its people live with the privations of hunger, as well as inadequate housing, education, and medical care. They look on as their environment is degraded and their resources are pillaged; as a result, there is an ever-growing population who look upon this nation's government, their government, with disdain and distrust. Our democracy has deteriorated to the point where people no longer feel as though the government will, or even can, respond to their most heartfelt concerns. And if a government cannot do this then truly it is not a good government, and it is only good governments that should be promoted and perpetuated; bad governments should not. It really is that simple.

Aristotle argued correctly that we are social animals, and we create governments as a function of this social propensity. But the critical piece of this statement that we often seem to disregard is that we created this entity called government to act on our behalf, and at our behest, to protect and serve the public good in the best possible way. Its mandate is not to serve primarily as a purveyor of favors to the rich, or to corporations, or to unions, or to the poor. On the contrary, the government is merely a tool, one that is meant to be under our control, to be used in shaping into reality our collective priorities. A government that does not act according to the informed will of the people serves to undermine its whole reason for being. Such a government, moreover, destroys its sole and ultimate source of legitimacy. No longer is it the purveyor of the public good, but rather, it is an impediment to such a good, and therefore, illegitimate.

In recent years, it has become increasingly obvious that the government does not serve the public good, but only that of a few private interests. A great many Americans believe this to be true, and as an outgrowth of this sentiment, believe the government no longer serves them. If a government is to claim that it represents the people, it must do just that: represent the people and their interests. If it is going to exclusively represent corporate interests it should be up front about its intent to do so, allowing the American people to do away with it and create a republic based upon the principles of the public good. But therein lies the problem; the whole institution of governance is underpinned with the perpetuation, not discontinuation, of its power. Aside from the obvious notion that it would legitimize the grievances that conclude it is not serving the public interest, the government cannot confront the public with its affront to the public good for the very reason that it believes it is already serving the public good. In the meantime it is persistent in doing wrong by the public in a very indiscreet manner, and it is for this reason that the public must assert its power to reclaim *res publica* in governance.

Certainly, in the eyes of Paine, the government under which we are subjects is not a good one; nor by definition is it a republic. Instead, this system of governance more accurately fits Carl Schmitt's characterization of a demagogic plutocracy. A demagogic plutocracy is a system that is effectively governed by the wealthy interests, be they individual or incorporated. It serves and maintains the interests of the wealthy, but it operates as though it were a system "of the people, by the people, and for the people." It is a system that appeals to the basest instincts of the masses by informing them that if they would only work longer and harder, they, too, could be affluent and influential, when it is altogether evident that this is not the case. It is a system that is both subtle and effective because it serves to convince the public that the current paradigm of governance serves the public good, while in actual fact it serves primarily the interests of a few affluent vested interests.

A great many of the citizens of this country are no longer fooled by the dog and pony show that the government puts on, apparently for our favor. This is altogether too clear when the government institutes policies that favor not the people, but rather the corporate interests that guide the plutocratic structure. Who, that would allow our schools to be rat-infested and decrepit, allow our country to boast the highest rates of poverty and imprisonment in the industrialized world, or give tax relief to the rich while they cut social programs for the poor, could claim that they were governing with *res publica* as their guiding principle?

These are not the actions of one person, or a group of persons, but the inertia of a long-deteriorating state of governance vis-à-vis the public good. More so than ever, the rise of the corporate state has begun to reveal itself for what it is. In a democracy people supposedly have real alternatives, have a voice, and wield a great amount of influence. But in this system, dominated by corporate interests, we see none of this but for the dogs and ponies prancing for our enjoyment. What we see instead is a system that is not, for all intents and purposes, democratic, nor is it governed by the public good for that matter; it is a government that is itself governed by corporate interests at the expense of its people.

As David Emory so aptly describes: In the current structure, people find that they are sitting on a tack, a rather sharp protrusion that violates their rump. If you have ever sat on a tack, you know what he means—and given my own experience of such a thing, I should hope that you have not, as it is far from pleasurable. In fact, it is not only extremely painful, but it is also altogether outside of our expectations of what we should experience when we sit down. This only serves to heighten the extraordinary distress we feel about this sensation. If we were to act out of our own will, it is clear that we would remove the tack with all due immediacy. Thus, one could say with relative assurance that such people would be acting in accord with their true will. Furthermore, more thoughtful people would take the extra precaution to ensure that there were no more tacks where they were about to sit, and that the one they just extracted from their rear would not be returned to this inconvenient locale.

A system that truly espouses a democratic republic would be much the same. First of all, the ideal in such a system is that there would never be a policy that would undermine the public good because in the forum for government there would be representatives that would wholeheartedly serve to realize the public good through thorough and thoughtful discussion and compromise. François Guizot's maxim states that government "is accordingly the place in which particles of reason that are strewn unequally among human beings gather themselves and bring public power under their control." Thus, through discussion, one would presume that reason should prevail and that public good would be served as an outgrowth of such discussion.

Yet, as Guizot's contemporary Robert von Mohl points out, there is really no guarantee that the particles of reason that have been unequally strewn throughout society are going to fully reassemble themselves in the body politic. There is always the possibility that the particles of reason necessary to reveal the truth of the matter with regard to the public good are not present within the governing body. Furthermore, what guarantee is there that the people who are best qualified for governing the nation are in fact being elected to positions of representation? Who, indeed, can say if they are even choosing to run? It is clear that in a system where the governance grows increasingly crooked, a good number of honest and qualified citizens who might otherwise run for office often do not because of the wretched condition of the government. This has the additional effect of accelerating the degradation of the system's integrity.

Thus, the further governance moves away from *res publica*, the greater is the repulsion of many citizens who are essential for delivering it back into the service of the public good. Consequently, the system is reinforced and made increasingly impregnable to the onslaught of concerns that the public good is not being considered, much less actively promoted. Such a structure, far from endeavoring to remove the tack from the rear ends of its public, seeks to convince the people that they must continue to sit upon it. Not because they are told to per se, but because it is "in their own best interest" to continue to sit on this painful artificial appendage. This argument has proved to be a convincing one, for the people continue to sit upon the tacks of poverty, of underfunded institutions of education, of inadequate healthcare, of environmental degradation, of the squandering of precious resources, of corporate greed, of financially irresponsible governance, of the gluttonous military-industrial complex, of racial injustice, of the imprisonment of nonviolent offenders, of continuous encroachments on personal freedoms in the name of national security, ad infinitum.

The people of this country possess bottoms that are readily becoming very tender, or callused, pincushions. For a long time people have been willing to accept the idea that there is a certain degree of suffering to be endured so that the American dream, which remains all but closed to them, does not vanish entirely from their purview. They have been willing to sit upon the tacks that are apparently the penance for the possibility of their future success. It is increasingly obvious, however, that the poor, with few exceptions, remain so, while the affluent, with few exceptions, continue to stay in their station. The only mobility seems to lie in the ever-shrinking middle class, and even that trend is not an upward one. The middle class is falling increasingly behind in its ability to maintain the standard of living that the middle class of thirty years ago enjoyed. And so, while the middle class shrinks, it also sinks. As the weight of the impending paucity of the middle class settles into the economic structure of the future, the increasingly bottom-heavy nature of this system serves only to intensify the pressure upon the tacks that underlie it. So tender have the supple and forgiving buttocks of the people grown that they are no longer willing to sit upon the innumerable tacks; it is, as Emory belayed, far too "taxing."

If the government does not take the necessary measures to free its people from the trappings of their wretched condition, then it is only a matter of time before that government is dispensed with. The people, quite simply, will rise and pluck themselves free of the quills they have too long endured. If this is to be done peacefully then there needs to be a dramatic shift in consciousness in both the public mind and in the structures and principles of governance in this country. It is my hope that this treatise will help to affect peaceful change in this regard, and falling short of this goal, then I hope at least it will provoke an honest discussion about who we are as a nation, and who, or what, we wish to become.

If this nation is to survive its ascendancy to the acme of world influence, it must radically alter its course. If it is to transcend the inevitable decline that befell all the world powers that have preceded it, this country must learn to promote, support, and develop the full potential of every individual within it. For if we are ever to realize, in the words of Neale Donald Walsh, "the grandest version of the greatest vision we ever held about who we are," we must begin an honest investigation of our beliefs, values, and priorities as individuals and as a people. The changes that so many people wish to see cannot be accomplished by way of our current path. It must be achieved through the ascendancy of *res publica* as the guiding principle in this new millennium.

The Legacy of Res Publica

"I've been to the mountaintop....
And I've seen the promised land.
I may not get there with you.
But I want you to know tonight,
that we, as a people will get to the
promised land."

— Martin Luther King Jr.

A s Martin Luther King Jr. articulated in his last speech, often called the *I See the Promised Land* speech, in the journey ahead of us, "we've got some difficult days ahead." Change is never easy, nor is it entirely painless, simply because we are comfortable in, and comforted by, the familiar even when it is not in our interest to embrace it. It is easy to continue to consume fossil fuels and difficult to find alternative renewable energy sources. It is easy to perpetuate the Horatio Alger mythology that tells us we, too, will be rich if only we work harder, and difficult to activate social policies that promote economic equity. It is easy to continue to invigorate the economy by funding the military-industrial complex, and difficult to find better ways to both infuse the economy with life and promote peaceful conflict resolution. It is easy to lock criminals away in a prison system, and difficult to grapple with the reasons people commit crimes or to rehabilitate and reintegrate

41

them—our system bothers with neither. It is much easier for us to continue perpetuating the current systems we have created because coasting on our inertia seems, at first glance, to require very little energy from us. And much like Newtonian physics, our society will stay in motion along the same path until it is acted upon by an outside force. While it may seem easier, this inertia takes its toll on all of us.

You do not have to be a person of great vision to see that our government is overrun by special interests, or that our environment is in danger, or that concerns over poverty, underemployment, the environment, and healthcare are coming to a head in this country. The face of the future is glaring right at us and we have critical choices to make in the coming years. As a species, we are on a path to self destruction. It may not be tomorrow, or a year from now, or even a hundred, for that matter. Still, one cannot deny that humanity simply cannot sustain our current practices and hope that the human race will be provided for eternally.

As a teacher, I was taught the "If-Then" methodology, which is used to help reinforce with students the idea that their actions have consequences, be they positive or negative. It is utterly essential that we continue to reinforce in ourselves that our actions have consequences, ones that are infinitely more terminal than those of a student who has not done their homework or has cheated on a test. The discretion we employ and the endeavors we embark upon will prove most definitively to be our legacy. The question that remains to be answered, however, is whether they will be reflected upon by future generations with grateful awe or contemptuous shame.

Let us cease and desist the journey we have embarked on upon our current path, for it is one that we are rapidly growing beyond. *If* we do not, *then* we continue at our peril. The millennium portends millennial change, and that must be our charge. In the coming years there is much we must do, and we've got some difficult days ahead, but it is essential that we press on in spite of the obstacles we face. Much will depend not only upon the diligent and sensible work of people from all walks of life, which is in itself essential to any and all great movements, but also upon the political and moral courage of politicians and plebeians alike to stand up for what is right, even if it is unpopular with those who most benefit from the existing establishment.

It is only when those whom we have empowered with the responsibility of governing this great country take it upon themselves to ensure the equality of freedoms, rights, and protections to all natural persons in this country, and abroad, that we can hope to live in a world where true and actualized freedom, equity, peace, and security carry the day. So long as corporations, militaries, and economies remain the moral compass of national standing in the world, there will be limited justice, restricted freedom, fleeting peace, and only partial equity. A world devoid of the spirit of *res publica* is not fit for humanity; the time has come when we must no longer turn a blind eye to the world, when we must create the change we wish to see. It is up to us, as Mahatma Gandhi implored, to be the change we wish to see.

Thus, let me declare on behalf of the people of this country, and of the world, that we shall insist upon governance where the interests of the people are the whole and sole purpose of governance. Let it be such that we, the people, demand no less than the full realization of the rights which govern the highest interest of the public good:

1. The Right of Primacy
2. The Right of Life, Health, and Security
3. The Right of Peace
4. The Right of Social Equity and Opportunity
5. The Right of Expanded Democracy

These shall no longer remain alien abstractions to us. On the contrary, they are the foundations of our future, and we will work tirelessly toward these goals until which time they are realized. Each is essential, indivisible, and dependent on the others.

The Right of Primacy

Governments exist so as to serve the people they govern, not the reverse. As such, we must demand that the impediments to its service of the public good be removed.

First, the greatest single threat to the primacy of the people in this country are large corporations. Thus, it is of supreme importance that corporate influence of any kind be removed from governance, whereby corporate personhood is revoked and its financial contributions to politics of any sort are made illegal. Currently, corporations have been guaranteed the same rights as citizens of the United States; they are protected by the Bill of Rights (organizations like unions, charities, and non-profits do not, by the way, have these rights guaranteed to them). Thus, corporations can make contributions to political parties because they have the right to freedom of speech. Government agencies cannot make surprise inspections of factories and plants to ensure that safety and sanitation standards are being observed, because corporations have are protected against "unreasonable"—read surprise—inspections. Yet, corporations, which have no natural mortality, bear few of the same responsibilities that individuals do. If they are found guilty of crimes, people at their helm are often charged, but the corporation continues unabated. When the actions of corporations knowingly result in the deaths of our country's citizens, there is no corporate death penalty to which private citizens are subjected for the same crime.

The Constitution was designed to protect this country's denizens, to provide them with a sling against the goliaths of government and business. The designers of the constitution recognized that the people are the first victim to fall prey to tyranny, and they require the means to defend themselves. But, as Thom Hartmann points out, if you give the people's cudgel to big business as well, then what chance do the people have against their vast wealth, power, and influence upon the government; very little, in fact. Thus, it is urgently important that we disarm the corporations and reserve the rights within the Bill of Rights only for natural persons. Thom Hartmann's *Unequal*

Protection: The Rise of Corporate Dominance and the Theft of Human Rights provides an excellent primer for resolving this difficulty.

Second, the global free trade agenda must be reformulated so as to ensure the protection and persistent progression of labor, cultural, economic, and environmental criteria such that the highest standards expected by any one nation be extended worldwide. Our country must devote itself to the promotion of responsible trade. What I cannot understand is how shortsighted corporations have become in their global trade agenda. When corporations race out of advanced countries in order to exploit those countries that have poor standards, they create international pressures of competition that drive down wages, and thus the purchasing power, of workers worldwide. Henry Ford understood nearly a hundred years ago that if he raised the wages of his workers they would be better able to purchase the products they produced. Yet, the current competition for jobs on the world market does the opposite. Beyond the immediate effects upon the worker, this current global dynamic serves to denigrate existing environmental standards and makes their progression increasingly difficult. The government of the American people, and of those around the world, must work to ensure that this race to the bottom for the workers of the global community is brought to an end. In its place, we must create a system that uplifts the standards of economic practices for all the world's citizens.

Third, the government and community must create the conditions necessary to facilitate the transition of media ownership and operation from private corporations to public media institutions, wholly independent of corporate or governmental influence. The media is the most sacred of democratic institutions. It is the primary tool used in providing citizens of this country with information about issues that matter to them. Yet, when this tool is wielded by the government or large corporations, the danger of its misuse is far too great. It is necessary for the development of a fully informed public that access to the airwaves is not restricted to the highest bidders. Rather, they should be reserved for a diverse range of not-for-profit, publicly funded institutions that are more widely controlled by the local media than is currently the case. The control of this precious resource should not be trusted to the corporate or political elite.

The Right of Life, Health, and Security

The rights to life and happiness are written into the Declaration of Independence, but the formula for happiness relies on the foundations of natural rights that are much more fundamental still: Health and Security. Without one's health or security of person, there is little time to consider one's happiness, unless it is in relation to one's relative lack of it. Thus it must be such that *res publican* governance be focused on ensuring that the citizens of this country be given the best possible tools for securing their health and welfare.

People are quite literally sick, to death in some cases, as a result of a system of healthcare and insurance that pays homage to the almighty dollar rather than to the sacred oath of Hippocrates. I believe most firmly that to do nothing when something can be done to save a life, or restore a person's health, is to do willful harm to them. To divert limited funding from cancer research to investigate and market male enhancement drugs is a willful and shameful abuse of very limited resources. Admittedly, being able to have sex when you're sixty is desirable, but it is far from essential, especially when you weigh the alternatives of life and death diseases of the body and mind. I have no knowledge of anyone dying from lack of an erection.

What are far more detrimental to people's health and welfare than any other single factor are the insurance companies that not only bar access to adequate medical treatment to millions of Americans, but also prevent them from obtaining affordable insurance against disasters with "acts of God" clauses. I urge any insurance company to prove the guilt of God in a court of law. They also serve to stymie the efforts of upstanding citizens from collecting on policies wherein they have dutifully fulfilled their obligation by paying their monthly premiums. Beyond their often shady practices, the insurance industry siphons off billions of dollars in funds used to maintain gross bureaucracies that could otherwise be used to further the development of medical and pharmaceutical technologies, expansion of service, or the reconstruction of people's lives and properties following unforeseen disasters. When profit takes precedence over that of the health and welfare of this country's greatest asset, its people, we have a serious problem. Thus, we must endeavor to disconnect the health and welfare, pharmaceutical, and insurance services away from the for-profit model.

Another important facet of people's health is the environmental standards to which our country's industries are held. Not only does the government have the power to regulate what chemicals can be pumped into our ecosystems, but it also has the power to regulate that which gets pumped into our systems through the food we eat. When we allow our government to be lax in the standards they set through the Environmental Protection Agency, the Food and Drug Administration, and other regulatory bodies, we are permitting them to give the green light to would-be polluters. In the end we all suffer the ill effects of a poisoned commons. We must insist that the government make the environment an immediate priority in the years to come.

The Right of Peace

It is hard to separate health and peace, for they are so intrinsically linked. War is the ultimate destroyer of health and security. Yet peace is possible; indeed it is imminent. While it is often such that the media projects images of what seems to us like an increasingly violent world, it is in fact the opposite. The United Nations recently released a document explaining what they termed the "Peacekeeping Paradox" whereby more and more countries who typically would have entered into indefinitely long and bloody conflicts to determine the supremacy of a political body, an idea, and so on, are now suing for peaceful alternatives, such as UN-sponsored peacekeeping missions. The problem is that there are not yet enough peacekeepers to fit the bill. Still, it is revelatory to recognize the global trends away from violent conflict.

Peace activism, too, has begun to undertake a dramatic shift. It has traditionally focused its energies on preventing war, rather than creating peace, in the hopes that peace will emerge from such protests. However, peace is not the absence of war; war is the absence of peace. In light of my favorite sport, hockey, allow me to indulge in an analogy. A team that seeks only to stop the opposing team from scoring can never hope to take the lead in a game, nor can they ever hope to win it; the best they can hope for is to maintain the status quo—a tie. It is only through the pursuit of one's own goals, and in defense of those that run counter to them, that the team can seek to win. Now, this is not to say that there are winners and losers in the process of seeking peace. It is quite the contrary, in fact. When we live in a secure, stable, and peaceful world, everyone will benefit duly. Yet, the fact remains that individuals and groups must seek to create peace if they want it to exist. The foundations for peace must exist for it to supplant our existing mode of being.

Organizations such as the North American Peace Alliance, the Global Renaissance Alliance, and others like them, along with some very dedicated individuals and politicians, are spearheading a campaign across the country to create a federal Department of Peace. This movement serves to advance peace, rather than to hold back the floodwaters of war. The Department of Peace is only one possible avenue to advance this cause in a proactive way, but it is one that will promote the education, voice, and the power of policy decision making both domestically and internationally, which can develop in us the sense of peace as a priority, as a policy, as a way of being, not simply the state of war's absence.

The most crucial, and most difficult, step in creating lasting peace is the dismantling of the military-industrial complex. This cannot simply take the form of a complete destruction of this complex; that would prove disastrous on many levels. On the contrary, the government must take rapid and calculated steps to transition from an economy based upon the military-industrial complex to one founded upon an enviro-industrial complex, whereby the focus of development is the improvement of methods, services, technologies, and products that replace or enhance existing ones to ensure the world's progress is environmentally, socially, and economically sustainable. Whereas now, in contrast, the developments are focused on that which can be destroyed. The change has the potential to produce and proliferate progress that maintains, sustains, and creates for the future of mankind.

That is not to say that militaries will cease to be necessary. I for one am not so naive to believe that we will all just throw down our weapons and be our brothers' keepers, regardless of how much I would embrace that if it were to occur. Yet, the changing global political requirements of military personnel are beginning to shift away from traditional national-security-based militaries to human security forces focused on the maintenance and protection of human interests worldwide. This transition is essential to building peace worldwide. Under the human security model, issues of domestic and international security are addressed on the level of the roots of violence, instability, and insecurity, rather than hedging against the predictable effects of such conditions. There is a valuable role for trained paramilitary peace-forces, which can more than offset the displacement of military personnel, to forward the goals and promises of peace worldwide.

The Right of Social Equity and Opportunity

It is important to the well-being of any society that there be a healthy degree of social equity. The greater the gaps between the wealthiest and poorest citizens of a country, the more crime and violence the society must deal with. When a person is struggling to feed and clothe their family while others live extravagant lifestyles, it is easy to understand why there will be a higher degree of social animosity and dysfunction. If I think about what might make me turn to violence to resolve what cannot be done through equity and justice, it would be to watch my family suffer without hope that our circumstances would ever improve. While I would hope never to embrace violence, and I certainly do not espouse it, I do understand why people turn to it out of desperation and sheer frustration.

The first important step necessary to facilitate the building up of greater equity in society is the restructuring and simplification of the tax system designed to reflect equity and the public good. In this restructuring, the lowest tax bracket would be raised to the level of a living wage for a family of four. If you do not make the amount of money experts decide is necessary to support a family of four at a level well above subsistence, you should not have to pay any taxes. Furthermore, all efforts should be made to ensure that every wage earner is able to meet this basic living wage. Deductions and loopholes must be thoroughly eliminated to rid the system of legislation specially tailored to favor certain sectors of society. It should resemble a progressive flat tax. If you make a certain amount of money, you should pay a certain percentage of your income, period. Yet, these taxes should be such that they serve to right the economic imbalances inherent in capitalism. Those that reap the greatest benefits of the economic system should also expect, and be expected, to contribute the greatest amount back into the common weal. Inheritance taxes, the so called "death tax," may be used as a case in point. There is a common misconception that each person who dies has to pay this tax. It is simply not true; in fact, this was never the case. This tax is only set to apply to those who have accumulated vast wealth. There are real concerns that family farms could suffer because of it, and to mitigate these worries, the tax should only apply to assets over and above an exemption of, say, five million dollars or ten million dollars (to pick an arbitrary number). Few Americans will ever see asset totals of this kind. Thus, the inheritance tax helps to balance out exorbitant wealth that a person has accumulated in their lifetime, using it instead to benefit the common weal.

A second initiative that should be introduced to reduce the burden of common citizens is known as a Pigouvian tax structure. What that means is that when companies produce, extract, or use commodities, materials, or resources that negatively affect the public, then they are subject to specialized taxes that are used not only to reimburse the country for destructive practices, but also to promote the development of more responsible alternative practices, products, and procedures. The greater the perceived harm to the environment, community, or citizenry is, the more the tax is increased. Not only will corporations become more readily amenable to practices that are environmentally and socially responsible, but it will also help to spur on the new enviro-industrial complex, thus easing the economic transition from war production to peace production. The wonderful aspect of this tax is that it tends not to affect individual small businesses that generally have less impact on the environment and targets instead large corporations that exploit and degrade the common space that communities of all sizes have to share.

While the tax system is of great importance in the creation of an equitable society, it is only one facet of a much larger program of social development. For any lasting change to exist, our country must have the courage to garner new resources, as well as better utilize those that we already have, to revolutionize American education. A nationwide educational revolution (NER) is currently on standby. There is an enormous body of research that propounds the myriad ways that education can be improved in this country. The national, state, and local governments, in partnership with business and community, must focus a massive reinvestment in education at all levels that ensures fully funded, radically diverse, and interest-specific, life-long educational opportunities for all individuals. The NER requires a complete reorganization of the structure of schooling based upon performance, interests, and development of students in small learning environments. Our current drive to force students to meet arbitrary standards and assessments without the resources to do so is an absurd abomination; it is an insult to anyone who is serious about improving education in any meaningful way in this country.

It is true that while small schools cannot always fulfill needs such as sports and a diverse array of elective opportunities, they do tend to produce far more impressive academic and personal growth results. In partnership with these schools, communities can work to develop extracurricular programs that small learning environments cannot otherwise support. As such, students can have access to these activities programs and have access to the best learning environment for them. By creating small learning communities a society enables its students to have greater choice in what they learn and how they develop, but most of all, it empowers students to be successful in ways that the cookie-cutter schools do not allow them to be. An empowered people are a creative, productive, and happy people. We must bring the factory system of education to an end. There are far better alternatives that have proven themselves to be tried and true.

The government can further the empowerment of its people through a system of social coordination. It should act to bring together the most successful strategies, programs, and ideas in order to expand them throughout the nation. We must also give communities the flexibility to adjust and tailor these initiatives to fit the special circumstances of their populations so that they may work that much better. The national coordination of what have come to be called "noospheric initiatives" is important in promoting that which is best in our society so that everybody may share in those successes. The term "noosphere," literally mind-sphere, was coined by Teilhard de Chardin, and elaborated upon in great detail by Barbara Marx Hubbard in *Conscious Evolution*. In this book she explained that by proliferating "golden innovations," or ideas that work magnificently in solving social problems such as crime, drug rehabilitation, obesity, educational deficiencies, and so on, we can have "a quantum effect in addressing a major social ill." *If* we have the power to coordinate and proliferate the ideas, programs, and initiatives that allow each individual to realize the grandest version of the greatest vision they have ever held about who they are, *then* we have an obligation to do so.

The Right of Expanded Democracy

The right to democracy, born of the ideals of the enlightenment, came to life in the American republic. America has long been the model for nations aspiring to democratic rule, yet we must recognize that our own development in this area still leaves much to be desired. Indeed, we have a great deal of work yet to do. Nearly half of the people who are eligible to vote do not. There are barriers to their voting that make it difficult, if not impossible, to get to voting stations, the registration process can often be confusing, and there is the simple explanation that mustn't be overlooked, namely that people are simply indifferent to the political processes of the country.

There is the very real sentiment among people in this country that the government does not represent them, but merely panders to the interests of big business. Many believe the choice between Republican and Democratic candidates akin to choosing between Tweedle-dee and Tweedle-dum. In many respects I agree with these sentiments, but where I must differ is in the belief in how important their vote is. It is true that politicians often do not serve us, but they do so because they know that we do not care enough to vote them out of office. So, we are left to contend with a perilous and vicious cycle. We don't vote because the government does not represent us; the government does not represent us because we don't vote. Ah, now what is one to do?

There are several solutions that I believe can serve to alleviate this conundrum. First, a no-voting penalty should be initiated. In order for a democracy to remain viable, it is necessary that its citizens participate in the political process. With the freedoms our democracy provides come the responsibilities of citizenship to which we must bind ourselves to ensure that our democracy remains robust. When you don't vote, your voice does not matter to the government, and they do not have to listen to you because they know that they cannot earn your assent when it comes to election day. Can they really be blamed in this? In the words of Civil Rights legend Vernon Dahmer, "If you don't vote, you don't count." That is not to say that people will be forced to vote. On the contrary, they would have the freedom to choose not to vote if they were willing to pay the no-vote penalty, which would be calculated on a sliding scale as a portion of their income.

There must, however, also be initiatives to ensure that all voters who desire to vote can do so. Many direct barriers to voting have been removed by the law such as grandfather clauses, poll taxes, and literacy tests; yet, there are institutional barriers that still exist, which we must endeavor to remove. The purging of voter rolls in Florida in 2000 or the disenfranchisement of people with criminal records are some of the most obvious barriers. But issues surrounding people physically being able get to the polls because of work requirements or transportation issues are also an area of major concern, as are the convoluted regulations regarding registration deadlines. These methods of hindering voter access to polling stations must be stricken from our democracy. Solutions could include a voter holiday, paid leave to vote, voter transit programs, automatic and on-site voter registration, an amendment to the constitution that forbids the disenfranchisement of American citizens from voter rolls for any reason; all these are part of a solution that helps to ensure that the opportunity to vote is available to all. It is only when all eligible voters can and do vote that our democratic tradition can be brought back to health.

Just as important for ensuring that democracies flourish is that there must be real alternatives between candidates. Unfortunately, the system we have built, far from fostering a variety of alternatives, has narrowed the choices penultimately. Effectively there are but two viable options in the United States: Republican or Democrat. This is a function of the electoral college; this system is set up so that any additional parties serve to hurt the party ideologically closest to them. Thus, the American people are faced with a decision not about who they most want to represent them in government; rather it is a vote against who they least want to be their representative.

While Americans are resistant to changes to their political system, the only solution I see if we do indeed want to create a political environment that provides Americans with real choices between candidates vying for political office is to replace an outdated and outmoded electoral college with a district-based (or even popular-based) proportional runoff system where candidates are eliminated until a single candidate receives a majority vote. A second election could be held, or more simply, voters could mark on their ballots the order in which they would like to see the candidates voted into office. If their candidate gets cut from the ballot for the runoff, their second choice is counted, then their third, and so on until the winner is determined. Electors can thereby vote their conscience without the usual worry that they might be "wasting their vote." Such an arrangement would eliminate pressures that prevent additional parties from running candidates, fostering for the American people real choice. Yet, this change would still maintain the integrity of the principles of governance that the country's founders instituted.

❧

While this is a humble beginning, we have critical decisions to make in the days and years ahead. And while it is true that many of our decisions will need time to prove sensible, we must not be afraid to give it to them so that they may bear us fruit, nor should we be too fearful or righteous to admit when they have not had the effect we have desired. We must all be aware that we will make our share of mistakes as we consciously remake our country and our world, and we must be prepared to take responsibility for them. For unlike the pristine condition of theoretical ideals, reality plays a role in shaping our ideas and our decisions in ways we cannot begin to understand in advance of our experience. Perhaps Mao Tse-tung put it best when he explained that "[in] a feudal society it was impossible to know the laws of capitalist society in advance because capitalism had not yet emerged, the relevant practice [i.e., industrialization] was lacking." So, too, it is impossible for me, or anyone for that matter, to know in exacting detail what the future will look like, and perhaps we are better off for it. Thus, we must be willing to admit to our failings and our weaknesses and move past them. If we cannot, then we will be forced to relive the expensive waste of our energies that our generation is currently experiencing.

Should we be compelled to recognize that we have been mistaken, we must have the strength of character to be able to amend our decisions, or make altogether new ones based upon our experience so that our goals, and not our egos, shall be satisfied. This is an essential element in the development of a new philosophy of governance for this millennium. In the words of

Joseph Addison, "When a man has been guilty of any vice or folly, the best atonement he can make for it is to warn others not to fall into the like." The same, I should think, holds true of societies, and indeed of governments. This notion is not an easy one to bear, because it requires a great deal of courage, honesty, and dedication toward *res publica* in governance, and while it seems today that this is in short supply, I have great faith in the capacity of our kind to realize this end.

What I desire above all else is that we take the initiative to begin this conscious evolution in a deliberate and unceasing manner so that we may realize the great reservoir of collective potential that humanity has to offer. Permit me entreat you that change is possible, and perhaps even imminent when the consciousness of the American people is aroused and mobilized. Let us create an environment wherein the American dream becomes the American reality for everyone who calls this great country home, and to all our brethren who span the globe. Let us alight once again the lantern of hope that America once held high upon the proverbial mountaintop as a beacon of promise for all the world to see. Let it render the impetus for the millennial revolution. We must, and we will. For if not us, then whom? And if not now, then when? Only when we have resumed the charge that this nation took upon itself more than two centuries ago will we fulfill the destiny to which we have laid claim: to assume the role of vanguard of human development to carry forth to the children of tomorrow the promise of a brighter future than the world we know today.

It is indeed a daunting task, for it must seem to us that the power elite have a stranglehold upon the structures that bind us to our positions in society. We are fearful, and kept this way, for it is the most powerful and also the last tool to be used in the suppression of change. Be it the media, or terrorism, or crime, or the perpetual stress of economic disaster, we have much that commits us to feeling as though we are perilously close to losing our grip on the edge of our existence. It is in serving the interest of the old order that we have much to lose, and need only to rock the boat for it to disappear in the chasm of history. In *The Culture of Fear*, author Barry Glassner explains, "The short answer to why Americans harbor so many misbegotten fears is that immense power and money await those who tap into our moral insecurities and supply us with symbolic substitutes." To me, this brings forth renewed meaning to Franklin Delano Roosevelt's promising words:

> So, first of all, let me assert my firm belief that the only thing we have to fear is fear itself—nameless, unreasoning, unjustified terror which paralyzes needed efforts to convert retreat into advance. In every dark hour of our national life a leadership of frankness and vigor has met with that understanding and support of the people themselves which is essential to victory. I am convinced that you will again give that support to leadership in these critical days. In such a spirit on my part and on yours we face our common difficulties.

Imagine that we cease to fear the phantasms that the power elite conjure up for us so that we might remain timid and thankful for their protection, imagine the change that could be made in the name of *res publica* if we fear not that we will be overwhelmed by the powers that be, imagine a world in which "we, the people" have regained the authority of the governance of this country, where the peoples of the world have regained the authority of their countries. Such a future is possible, if only we have the courage to choose it.

It is true, the structures and systems that exist must seem like mountains that will exist in perpetuity; they are monolithic obstacles in our conception of the world. Yet permit me to share with you the wise words of nineteenth-century orator Robert Green Ingersoll: "In the presence of eternity the mountains are as transient as the clouds." While the shattering of the earth may raise the mountains upward, the steady pounding of the elements erode and demolish them when their time has come. It is this transience that we must not only be cognizant of, but also use to give rise to progress. The force of the earthquake is tremendous indeed, but the effects of perpetual erosion are no less powerful. The systems that exist today, even in

57

their enormity, exist only because we had the power to build them up, and if it is such that we have the power to build them up, we, too, have the power to tear them down. The time has come to move into action so that we may build them anew in the spirit of *res publica*.

It is altogether too common to feel the daunting weight of change falling solely upon our own shoulders; it feels as though no one but ourselves desires the change we seek, and if they do, they are not willing to work for it. Yet, let it be known that the tide is rising and each man, woman, and child has a role to play in bringing about a system of good governance that is truly "of the people, by the people, and for the people," so that we may truly see *res publica* become a manifest reality. The power elite have force on their side, this much is true. They have a stranglehold upon the media, upon the economy, and upon the government. But we have a legitimate and undeniable advantage on our side. We are nearly three hundred million strong.

Imagine the enormous impact of even two hundred million handwritten letters (the most powerful of all lobbyists) falling upon the desks of Washington every month, without end, until our representatives began to pursue the spirit of *res publica* on behalf of the American public. Imagine the impact of *three hundred million* people around the country banging on the offices of their representatives, or storming to the polls, to demand in person that our government officials act upon the principles of *res publica*. Imagine the impact of millions of individuals making the pilgrimage to Washington to insist upon the call for *res publican* governance in the name of our people.

In the movie *Finding Nemo* there is a truly revolutionary scene in which a great many fish, including the title character, are caught up in a net and are floundering in an anarchic tumult as they are being pulled from the depths of the sea. Nemo, though with difficulty, manages to rally them to all swim in one direction, convincing them in a pseudo-Marxist fashion that if they do so they might just escape their impending demise. Convinced that they have nothing to lose but their nets, the fish dive down toward the ocean floor, breaking free from the trappings of their doomsday machine. When we are

divided against ourselves, we are as helpless against the machi-
nations of the power elite as the catch of the day is to the great
oceanic fishing trawlers. If, however, the American people act in
unison to demand that the politicians of this country serve the
people, and only the people, in the pursuit of *res publica* or face
the end of their political careers, they will listen; they will have
little choice.

We must doggedly engage in the peaceable, yet powerful,
means to these ends. For we have a choice: In the words of David
C. Korten in his contribution to Marianne Williamson's
Imagine: What America Could Be in the 21st Century, "We can resign
ourselves to an American-imposed corporate order that is reck-
lessly destroying the life of society and the planet to enrich a
small ruling elite. Or we can take on one of the greatest creative
challenges in history: consciously and intentionally to reinvent
ourselves and our institutions to create a planetary system of
democratic, self-organizing societies grounded in a love of life
and a respect for all beings. They lead to two sharply contrast-
ing futures." I believe the choice is clear for all to see; and in this
pursuit of *res publica*, we shall revolutionize the world.

Afterword

"We gotta make a change...
It's time for us as a people to start makin' some changes.
Let's change the way we eat, let's change the way we live
and let's change the way we treat each other.
You see the old way wasn't working so it's up to us to do
what we gotta do, to survive."

— Tupac Shakur

In the preceding chapters I have presented the world as I believe it to be—the problems that are standing in the way of our development as an equitable society, the philosophical imperative for the change I propose, and what I believe must be done to realize it. If it is such that my words speak to you, it is not that I am a soothsayer, nor is it because my ideas are new, nor that I have insight into the world that was previously lacking. On the contrary, it is simply that I have voiced what you already believe to be the truth. Alternately, if it is that my words do not speak to you, it is not because I am entirely wrong, nor because I am foolish or naive; and rather than dismiss them outright, I would challenge you to reflect upon why they sound to you like falsehoods. From both my supporters and detractors I would ask of them that they reflect honestly about what I am offering so that both may take from it what is useful to our development as a united people. I ask for nothing more than this.

If I produce another -ism, then I will have failed utterly; we are already all too often the victims of the -isms—communism, capitalism, racism, fascism, sexism...the list goes on and on. Like others before me who have looked to the future with a vision and a plan, there is much that can be done to get us there. My way is not the only way, it is but one route on the myriad paths of our being. The opening line of the *Tao Te Ching* describes this perfectly: "The Way that can be told is not an Unvarying Way." So while I speak in imperatives, I cannot know for certain what the future will hold, nor the true consequences of our actions. Prognostication has never been my favorite suit, nor, I suspect, my best one. I am not omniscient any more than the next person, and I refute notions that anyone possesses this quality as preposterous. Mao Tse-tung conveyed his contempt for the ideologue: "The most ridiculous person in the world is the 'know-all' who...declares himself 'the world's Number One authority'." Though I am no great fan of Mao, in this he speaks the truth. If that is my lot, or if I convey this impression, again I will have failed.

I do hope with all sincerity that what this work stands for will prove to be the impetus that drives us together to forever change our world. Take what you may from this manifesto, or dismiss my words, as you see fit. Yet, in whatever choice you make, realize that it is you, the people, that have the power to shape the future.

Printed in the United States
22952LVS00002B/10-24

9 781587 363757